Great Smoky Mountains National Park
Animals & Attractions

Billy Grinslott & Kinsey Marie Books

ISBN - 9781960612885

There are many animals in the smoky mountains national park. We have listed some of the more popular ones that are found and would be fun to see.

Chipmunks are found in many areas. Chipmunks are small members of the squirrel family. They like to eat nuts and seeds. They have pouches inside of their cheeks so they can carry food. They are very friendly and will take food from your hand.

There are many squirrels in the wild. You may see a red or gray squirrel. The most popular is the gray squirrel. Squirrels are very acrobatic and can climb trees. Their favorite food is acorns. They like to collect acorns and eat them later.

Flying Squirrels don't fly like birds. They don't have wings. They have skin that is attached to their legs. When they jump from a tree, they spread their legs out and glide through the air. Most glides are 30 feet from tree to tree. But they can glide up to 150 feet.

Fishers are native to North America. They hiss and growl when upset. They are closely related to badgers, mink, and otters. Fisher young are known as kits. Fishers are one of the few animals that eat porcupines. Fishers are also called pekan, pequam, wejack, and woolang.

Otters have the thickest fur of any animal. The otter is one of the few mammals that use tools. A group of otters resting together is called a raft.

Otters primarily rely on their sense of touch, whiskers, and forepaws, in murky waters to locate food. Otters have built in pouches of loose skin under their forearms to stash extra food when diving.

Groundhogs or woodchucks are the largest member of the squirrel family. Groundhogs get their name because of their big bodies, and they live underground. Groundhog Day is where Punxsutawney Phil predicts how long winter will last.

Pee-ewe what is that stinky critter with the big bushy tail. It smells bad. Skunks are normally curious and friendly unless you scare them. If you scare them, they will flip their bushy tale at you and spray you with a smelly potion and it stinks.

Opossums or possums have strong tails and can hang from trees. One trick that a possum has, is when it feels danger is it will play dead. It will lay there and not move. Possums have white to gray face hair. Possums like to eat wood ticks. They are also immune to snakebites.

Raccoons like to come out at night. Their eyes are made so they can see in the dark. They are called masked bandits because they have a dark mask around their eyes, and they like to raid and eat out of trash cans at night.

There are several types of foxes in North America. This is a red fox. Females are called vixens. Red foxes have supersonic hearing. When afraid, red foxes grin or look like they are smiling. Red foxes front paws have five toes, while their hind feet only have four. There are red and gray foxes in the smoky mountains national park.

The coyote is bigger than a fox. Eastern coyotes are part wolf. Coyotes are great for pest control. They like to eat mice and rats. They can adapt and live almost anywhere, even in the city. They have a yip type of call when they communicate with each other. Coyotes are found in all the United States, except Hawaii.

The timber wolf, also known as the gray wolf, is the largest wolf in North America. Wolves are legendary because of their spine-tingling howl, which they use to communicate. Their territory size is 25 to 150 square miles. They like to roam in packs of 2 to 25 wolves. You can see gray and red wolves in the smoky mountains national park.

The mountain lion is one of the biggest cats in North America. The largest mountain lion ever recorded weighed 276 pounds. Mountain lions don't roar like other big cats they communicate in different ways, such as chirping, growling, shrieking, and even purring.

Wild turkeys were almost extinct, now they can be found in most parts of North America. Only male turkey's gobble. Wild turkeys can fly. Wild turkeys sleep in trees. They can change colors. Turkeys can see better than humans. Turkeys can run up to 18 mph and can fly up to 50 mph. They are incredibly curious and inquisitive animals who enjoy exploring. Turkeys are highly intelligent animals.

Wild boars are part of the pig family. Wild boars have tusks on their lower and upper lips. The wild boar has long, rubbery snout that is used for digging for food. Wild boars are nocturnal animals, they come out at night. They are very family orientated and like to live in groups called sounds. They have a double coat of fur to help protect them.

Black bears are the smallest members of the bear family in North America. Black Bears love to eat sweet things like berries, fruits, and vegetables. They are good climbers and fast runners. They usually sleep for long periods of time and hibernate during the winter. They typically try to stay away from people.

The whitetail deer is the most popular deer in North America. Whitetail deer have good eyesight and hearing. Only male deer grow antlers, which are shed each year. Whitetail deer are good swimmers and will use large streams and lakes to escape predators. A young deer is called a fawn. They are the most common deer species and live everywhere in North America.

Weighing in at up to 700 pounds, the Elk is one of the biggest deer species on earth. They can run as fast as 40 miles per hour. They can outrun horses. They make a cool bugling sound when communicating with other elk. It's fun to listen to them. Only male elk have antlers. That they shed and regrow every year.

There are plenty of sights to see, and things to do in the Great Smoky Mountains National Park. We have listed the top attractions for the park.

Newfound Gap is the lowest drivable pass through the Great Smoky Mountains National Park. A trip on Newfound Gap Road has been compared to a drive from Georgia to Maine in terms of the different variety of forest you will see. It typically takes about an hour to drive, depending on traffic. The drive includes opportunities for you to stop and enjoy the scenery, like Newfound Gap overlook.

The observation tower on the summit of Clingmans Dome offers spectacular 360° views of the Smokies mountains and beyond. On most days you can see up to 20 miles. It is a steep half mile walk to reach the top of the observation tower. Clingmans Dome Road is seven mile long and it offers several scenic pull-offs, that offer awesome views of ridges and valleys along the way.

The narrow, winding Roaring Fork Motor Nature Trail lets you enjoy the forest and historic buildings of the area. The 5.5-mile-long, one-way road is a favorite trip for many people who visit the Smokies.

The Chimney Tops Trail is one of the most popular trails in the Great Smoky Mountains National Park. Because of its length and spectacular views. The trail gains 1,400 feet in nearly 2 miles which makes for a steep climb, be sure to wear sturdy shoes and bring plenty of water. The scenery on this hike is worth it.

Although Abrams Falls is only 20 feet high, the large volume of water rushing over falls makes up for its lack of height. The trail to the fall's goes through pine and oak forest on the ridges and hemlock forest along the creek. The hike is 5 miles roundtrip and considered moderate in difficulty.

Trillium Gap Trail runs through an old-growth hemlock forest and runs behind the 25-foot-high grotto waterfall. The cool, moist environment near the falls is ideal for summer hikers. The hike is 3 miles roundtrip and considered moderate in difficulty. Black bears are sometimes seen in this area.

Rainbow Falls Trail. A rainbow produced by mist from this 80-foot high waterfall is visible on sunny days. The 5.4 mile roundtrip hike is considered moderate in difficulty. The Rainbow Falls Trail continues for approximately 4 miles beyond the falls to the summit of Mount Le Conte.

Laurel Falls is 80 feet high. The waterfall has an upper and lower section, divided by a walkway crossing at the base of the upper falls. It's a popular destination. Parking at the trailhead is limited. The roundtrip hike to the waterfall is 2.6 miles and the hike is considered moderate in difficulty.

The trail to Cataract Falls is one of the best-kept secrets in the Smoky Mountains. This trail is only 3/4-mile roundtrip and suitable for families with young children. The trail starts directly to the left of the visitor center for easy access. This trail provides excellent views of 25-foot high Cataract Falls.

Ramsey Cascades is the tallest waterfall in the park and one of the most spectacular. Water drops 100 feet over rock outcroppings and collects in a small pool. The trail to the waterfall gains over 2,000 feet in elevation over its 8-mile roundtrip hike. Considered strenuous in difficulty. It follows rushing rivers and streams for most of its length.

The hike to Spruce Flats Falls in the Smoky Mountains begins from the Lumber Ridge Trailhead in Tremont. It is a 1.8-mile roundtrip hike. Generally considered a moderately challenging route. It's one of the nicer little waterfalls on the Tennessee side of the smoky mountains.

The Sinks area of the Smoky is one of the most fascinating spots along the Little River Road scenic drive. This roadside stop on the scenic Little River Road offers an incredible view of a waterfall and its pools of water. The Sinks formed where the river makes an S-turn creating natural pools that are outlined on both sides by humongous boulders.

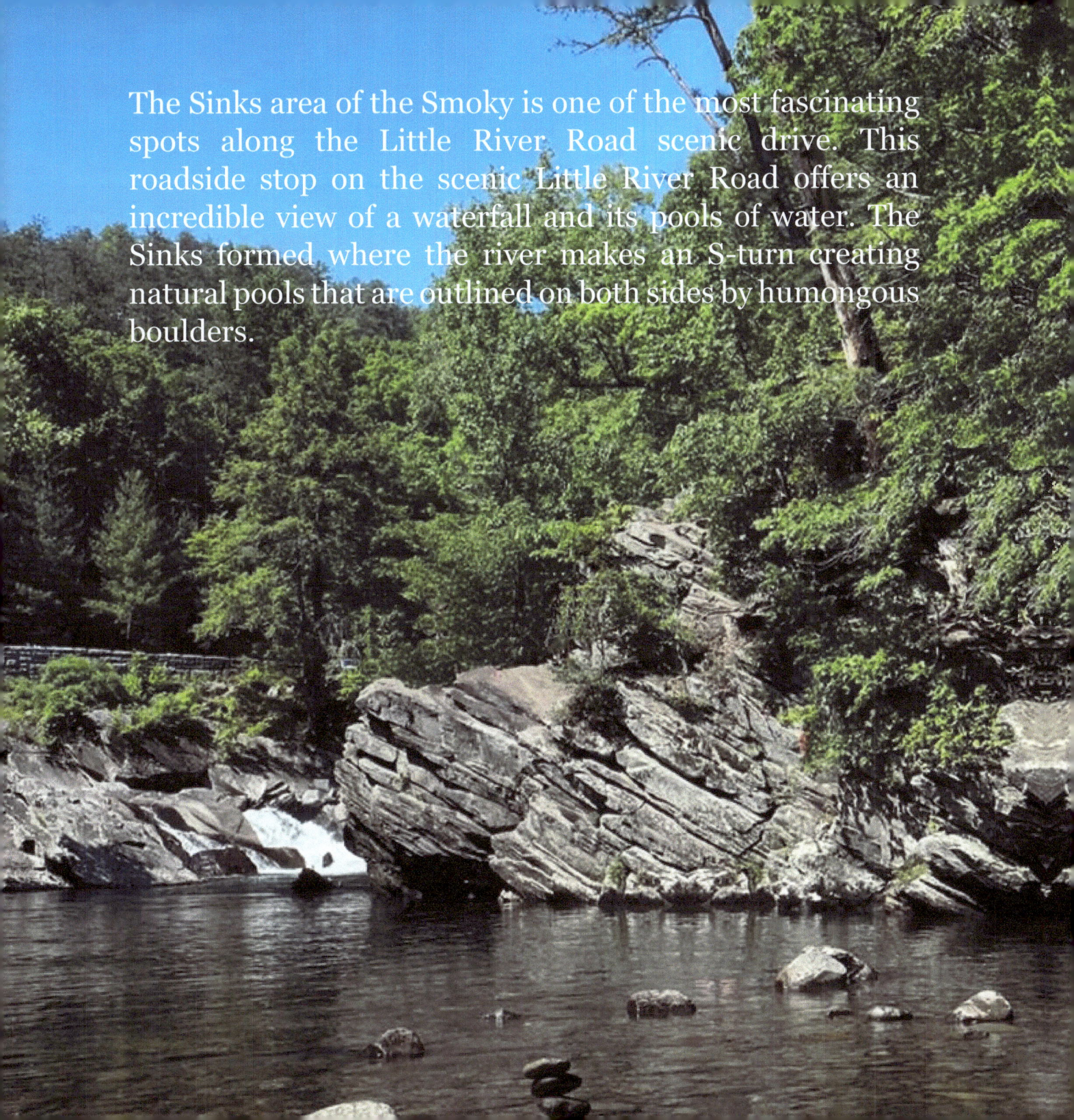

Cades Cove is a broad valley surrounded by mountains and is one of the most popular destinations in the Smokies. It offers some of the best opportunities for wildlife viewing in the park. Large numbers of white-tailed deer are seen, and sightings of black bears are also possible. An 11-mile, one-way road circles the cove, offering motorists the opportunity for an awesome sightseeing adventure.

Cataloochee Valley is surrounded by 6000-foot peaks. In 2001, elk were released in Cataloochee Valley to reintroduce elk to the park. The herd can be seen regularly in the fields of the valley, especially in the early morning and evening hours. Visitors to Cataloochee valley also enjoy viewing deer, elk, turkey, and other wildlife. This is the best place to see historic buildings from the late 19th and early 20th centuries.

Alum Cave Trail. The trail begins by crossing log bridges, leading hikers through an old-growth hardwood forest. Hiking through the tunnel of Arch Rock is a highlight of the hike. The Alum Cave Bluffs are 2.3 miles from the trailhead. This is a good place to view the rugged valley while surrounded by mountains.

Look Rock Trail has a lot to offer. Not only can you hike the short trail. It also offers a campground. Look rock has an observation tower you can easily hike to. The trail to Look Rock Tower is short and easy for all ages. The Look Rock Tower is a concrete observation tower that allows excellent views of the of the Great Smoky Mountains.

The Appalachian Trail is one of the nation's most spectacular hiking trails. It travels 72 miles through Great Smoky Mountains National Park following the Tennessee-North Carolina border. It takes an average of seven days to hike the full route, or you can start midway at Newfound Gap to reduce the distance by half.

Mount LeConte stands 6,600 feet tall and is the third highest peak in the Great Smoky Mountains National Park. It is a 13-mile roundtrip hike. The number of interesting sites and challenge of the trail is sure to amaze even experienced hikers. Whether you are an avid hiker on your next adventure or a tourist looking to make the most of your retreat, this trail could be your path to an exciting day of exploring.

Charlies Bunion Trail. Enjoy the breathtaking mountain views along the Appalachian Trail on this hike to a stone outcrop known as Charlies Bunion. Enjoy this 8.0-mile roundtrip trail near Gatlinburg, Tennessee. Generally considered a moderately challenging route, it takes an average of 5 hours to complete. This is a popular area for hiking. You will likely encounter other people.

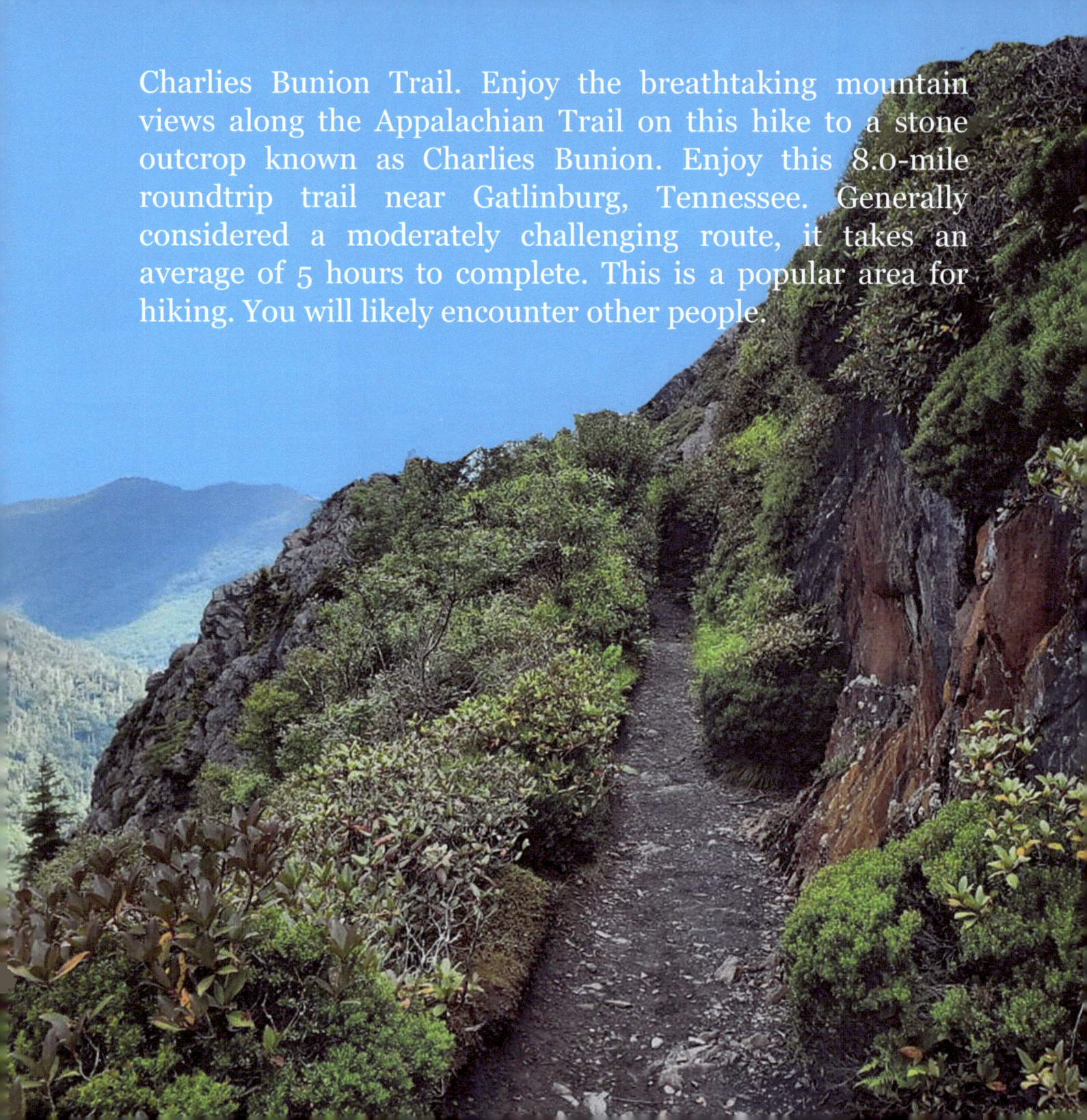

The foothills parkway has 33 miles of open road you can drive to view the smoky mountains. The southern section of the Parkway offers some spectacular views of the Smoky Mountains on one side and the Tennessee Valley on the other. There are several overlooks where you can see different mountain peaks. You can stop get at any of these pull offs.

Ways to Enjoy the Smoky Mountains Park

Scenic Driving Routes - Blue Ridge Parkway, Roaring Fork Motor Trail, Foothills Parkway. Little River Road, Upper Tremont Road, Cades Cove Loop Road.

Visitor Centers - Sugarland Visitor Center, Cades Cove Visitor Center, Oconaluftee Visitor Center.

Picnicking – They have plenty of picnic spots.

Camping – There are many camping spots in the smoky mountains.

Hiking – There's many sights to see by walking to them.

Biking – There are many places to bike in the park.

Swimming – Check with the park for safe areas to swim.

Fishing – There's many spots where you can fish.

Horseback Rides – guided rides are available.

Historic Buildings – Visit historic buildings or Elkmont ghost town.

Make your plans ahead of time, before going.

Author Page

Billy Grinslott & Kinsey Marie Books

ISBN - 9781960612885

www.ingramcontent.com/pod-product-compliance
Lightning Source LLC
Chambersburg PA
CBHW060850270326
41934CB00002B/74